G000065429

Beauty in the Chaos

31 Uplifting Devotions to Sweeten the Soul

by

Sam Silcock

ISBN: 9798723677975
Imprint: Independently published

Gracious words are like a honeycomb, sweetness to the soul and health to the body.

Proverbs 16 v 14
ESV

INTRODUCTION

'Beauty in the Chaos' is a phrase the Holy Spirit gave to me, whilst on a mission trip to Cambodia in early 2020, with Mission Direct. We were building a home for a family in Phnom Penh in partnership with Serve Cambodia. The traffic was crazy, market places buzzed and there were all sorts of sights, sounds and smells. You could say it was chaotic.

But amidst that chaos was beauty. I had offered to do the morning devotion one day and had been praying God would give me something to share. I felt him tell me it was the people that make a place. The people were beautiful. The Cambodians have been through terrible times, yet many of them showed such joy.

Life can often change unexpectedly. Mine was turned upside down when I went through a divorce, not something I ever thought would happen to two believers. Then along came the pandemic. Living alone, divorced, COVID19, whatever next?

I had started walking daily to clear my head. God also really began to speak to me in those times. I would get home and share it on Facebook. And so my Facebook page 'Sam's Life Encouragements' was born. I learnt to hear God's voice far more frequently in the simplest of things. As I walked I would see something, or be reminded of a song or an experience.

The encouragements in this book are an adaptation of my blog entries. They are real life. They are a testimony of God's faithfulness to speak, particularly in times of trouble. He has been my rock throughout these challenging times and he can also be yours. If we take time to listen, his voice can be clearer than we often perceive it to be.

And finally God loves vulnerability. Times of brokenness can lead us into his presence. If we allow it, we can become more dependent on him rather than our human nature. We can learn to experience joy even amidst the pain.

We can learn to see the 'Beauty in the Chaos'.

DAY 1 : LOVE NOT FEAR

I had seen the phrase 'love not fear' graffitied on a cliff face and it made me stop and reflect. I was sure it was a moment God had created for me to stop and think on my walk. It is very easy in this life to be consumed by fear. Perhaps a fear of the future or a fear of the past. Perhaps a fear of the present. And the sad thing is that fear can rob us of our joy and of the moment.

I know that anxiety has reared its ugly head in my life following my divorce, and then the nuisance of COVID19. It has been a battle for me, and fear is a battle for many of us. It can easily become a daily struggle.

1 John 4 v 18 (NLT) says:
'Such love has no fear, because perfect love expels all fear. If we are afraid, it is for fear of punishment, and this shows that we have not fully experienced his perfect love.'

That is a challenge for all of us. Are we willing to challenge the fears we have and allow them to be replaced by God's love instead? What are our fears based on?

Our past has gone and we cannot change it. We don't know what the future holds and we have a choice in the present. That verse demonstrates that it is when we grasp love, that we can let go of fear.

I know I have a way to go and perhaps you do too. But I am blessed that one piece of graffiti on a cliff face can be used to show such an important reminder. You are loved! And although it may be clichéd, "it's going be okay".

Along the coast path near Broadstairs, Kent.

DAY 2 : RENEW YOUR MIND

I had been doing some weeding at work. Perhaps not the most exciting task for some, but being sat in the glorious sunshine clearing a shingle path was surprisingly therapeutic. I spent time admiring the beautiful plants and enjoyed the various sounds of the birdsong.

My mind wandered and I thought about how our minds can become like that path of weeds. They can become clogged up with all sorts of worldly clutter, from tiny things with barely any roots to larger ones which are difficult to budge!

This was during a time of national lockdown, when many people were stuck at home with less to do. It definitely felt like an ideal opportunity had been given by God, to do some mental gardening. Sometimes we only need a little tidy up, but others we may need to get out the shovel and do some more serious business! Quieter moments or seasons in life are a prime time to do some alternative work and invest in yourself.

Romans 12 v 2 in the ESV says:
Do not be conformed to this world, but be transformed by the renewal of your mind, that by testing you may discern what is the will of God, what is good and acceptable and perfect.

Another verse in Colossians 3 v 2 tells us to set our minds on the things that are above and not on the things that are on earth.

And finally, what should we think about? The bible gives us a good answer for that one too. Philippians 4 v 8 says:

Finally, brothers, whatever is true, whatever is honourable, whatever is just, whatever is pure, whatever is lovely, whatever is commendable, if there is any excellence, if there is anything worthy of praise, think about these things.

I know I have a few things I need to clear up, how about you?

My prayer for you is that you will overflow more and more with love for others, and at the same time keep on growing in spiritual knowledge and insight, for I want you always to see clearly the difference between right and wrong, and to be inwardly clean, no one being able to criticize you from now until our Lord returns. May you always be doing those good, kind things that show you are a child of God, for this will bring much praise and glory to the Lord.

Philippians 1 v 9-11 (TLB)

DAY 3 : IMPACT

Impact. That's what I made as I stamped my foot into the sand on to the beach. Impact, as I wrote 2021 with my finger. I wanted to leave my mark, so I had stamped a footprint into the sand and written the year inside it. It had required two impacts, a big one and a smaller one. What amused me is that I had done that at the beginning of a walk, but got so distracted by my thoughts, that I forgot where I had left my mark! More on that shortly.

It was the beginning of 2021 and I was thinking about the previous year. If years were represented like wedding anniversaries, 2020 was toilet paper and we all know what that's used for! Humour aside, there had been good as well as bad. Back to those impacts. No doubt 2020 has left a negative mark on many. But what about the positive impacts? How about the unexpected blessing, a comment from a loved one, a gift, extra time or lessons learned?

As we journey through life things make a mark on us, they have impact. We also can have an impact on others. It doesn't have to be big all the time either. We live in a culture of pressure to do this and that, to perform well, etc. We are often hard on ourselves, I know I often have been. Your impact may be the big foot stamp in the sand, or the gentle writing with the finger, it does not matter which one!

The point is we are living for a great God and nothing we do is wasted. What matters is that we seek and use the opportunities we are given.

I had forgotten where I'd left my mark in the sand, but the impact itself was not forgotten. I had taken a photograph and still had a chance to use it. In the same way, you may forget the positive impact you may have had on others. BUT, they probably haven't forgotten the impact you had on them!

As we step into a new year, or a new season, let's remember we can still make a difference whatever our situation. Whether it's a smile given to a stranger or a big achievement, they both make a difference.

As the bible encourages us in Matthew 5:16:

In the same way let your light shine before others, so that they may see you good works and give glory to your Father who is in heaven.

Whether you're a tiny flickering tea light or a bright blazing floodlight, you are still shining in the darkness. Be blessed and shine as you walk your journey and remember your impact is never forgotten.

DAY 4 : GRACE

When I was younger I spent quite a lot of time writing poetry. I am the creative and expressive type and I would frequently write them and stick them in a folder. I used to dream they might one day end up in a book. Many years later they have escaped the folder and a few of them are in this book. One of those poems, 'Grace' is the theme for this encouragement:

Grace

Descending from Heaven like a peaceful dove
Gentle like a cooling breeze
Greater than any other love
Is your grace given unto me

Deeper than the deepest ocean
More vast than expanses of open arid land
More numbered than the stars in space
Are blessings flung from your hand

Flowing like a mighty river
With every part surrounding me
Roaring like a waterfall
Is your grace that covers me

We need to remember that human love is imperfect and will never match the standard of our loving Heavenly Father. Even the best love you have experienced on earth pales in comparison. Grace is so much deeper. Our real security is in the one who designed us and we need to learn, to let go of earthly things and embrace His love.

A short prayer

Heavenly Father, help us to embrace real love. Help us to let go of those things that distract us from who we were designed to be. Let us experience the freedom of knowing our identity is in you and that your grace surpasses all things.

Amen

My grace is enough; it's all you need. My strength comes into its own in your weakness

2 Corinthians 12 v 9 (The Message)

DAY 5 : THANKFULNESS

I had tuned in to watch the Prime Minister give his announcement to the nation. Another national lockdown. But as I was on my way home from my support bubble that evening, I thought about my job and how lucky I was to be in a secure position, and able to travel around and see people at work. Opportunities to interact had changed for everybody in some way.

It was very tempting with all that was happening, to moan. We Brits are very good at it, often adding hatred and cynicism to the mix. I wonder how many had insulted the PM. Not me. Why? Because we were fortunate really. We could have had far worse. For a man who has a family and had been through COVID himself I think the PM did alright. I wonder how different his life would be if the media and the population were grateful instead of critical?

Times have been tough for many. As I edit this, we are nearing the end of the lockdown in March 2021. Despite circumstances, there are always things we can be grateful for. Parents or guardians, a reliable car, food in the kitchen and a home, to name a few. If you are concerned for others who are struggling, then you have an opportunity to get alongside them.

Our difficulties are only for a season and we can be thankful throughout them. 1 Thessalonians 5:18 (NIV) says:

Be thankful in all circumstances, for this is God's will for you who belong to Christ Jesus.

So I encourage you to show someone some gratitude. You will bless them greatly and it may just bless you too!

PRAY

Lord Jesus

Help me to be thankful in all circumstances. Help me to see your provision and have my eyes open to see what you are doing. Thank you that you are good to me, you are always faithful. Give me an attitude of gratitude and strength for all I face.

Amen

DAY 6 : THE WAY

As we travel through the journey of life we can face many hardships. Hindsight has always revealed that it is God who has got me through. In my experience he has got me through depression, kept me alive when I was suicidal and healed me from the shattering pain of a divorce. And that only covers a few of my 38 years!

We need to be real about these things, we need to talk about them and essentially we need to listen to them without judgement or presumption; particularly in the spiritual context.

Below is a poem I wrote about the goodness of God. It is not intended as a super-spiritual application or blanket prescription which magically wipes away our problems! It is a declaration of the character and goodness of God. We will always have hardships and will probably never grasp all of the truths mentioned.

As you read it, be encouraged that you are not alone in your difficulties. There is light at the end of the tunnel and a faithful God who cares for you throughout your journey.

So here it is, 'What would I have done?'

There was a time when I was blind, but he gave me eyes to see
A time when I was helpless, but he came and helped me
When I was friendless, He became my friend
I was hopeless, now I have hope

And I was lost, so He came and found me
What would I have done if it wasn't for Jesus?
I was hell-bound, now I'm heavenward
I was broken and He restored me
I was ignored, so he loved me
I was sick and He healed me

What would I have done if it wasn't for Jesus?
I cried and He cried with me, then He wiped the
tears away
I would hide, but He always found me
Now I know He is the way
He died for me, but then He rose again

What would I have done if it wasn't for Jesus?
He forgave me for my sins, when His blood washed
them all away
He promised me eternal life and that in His arms I'd
stay
How I love you my saviour Jesus!

DAY 7 : WHAT ARE YOU LIVING FOR?

I opened my Google news feed on my phone to have a quick look at what was going on. I don't tend to spend too long doing so, I just take small 'doses' for awareness of what's going on in the world!

One article in particular got my attention. Elon Musk had become the world's richest man to the tune of £136bn, ahead of Amazon CEO Jeff Bezos. What grabbed my attention is what Musk stated he would use the money for. Half to help with 'problems on Earth' and the other to develop Mars in case of doom on earth. His response? 'Back to work'.

Interesting. It's good to be driven and have ambition or even fulfil a dream if you're fortunate enough. There's some very clever entrepreneurs out there; our lives are probably better because of them. But if you or I were to be in his position with that kind of wealth, what would we do with it?

I admire his vision, but I but perceived an underlying fear. 'Problems on Earth' were likely a reference to climate change. His reasons for Mars development included things like a meteor hitting Earth and World War 3. Woah!

I wonder what could be achieved if he was investing in Heaven instead of Mars? I was reminded that I am not living for the things of this world. I sure screw up plenty of times and like many of us have a long way to go. But Musk's 'back to work' comment implies that those plans for the money are his driving force.

I want my driving force to be my Creator and my actions to be contributing towards my rewards in Heaven. When I wake up each day, my desire is that I would be like Christ. Well, that's what I aim for at least! I want to build others' up and represent Him well in all that I do. I want what I do to point towards Heaven (not Mars).

If we live for another agenda, it will always be a case of 'back to work'. There is nothing wrong with a strong work ethic or earning well, but we need to think about what or who we are working for! Colossians 3:23-24 (NLT) says:

Work willingly at whatever you do, as though you were working for the Lord rather than for people. Remember that the Lord will give you an inheritance as your reward, and that the master you are serving is Christ'.

And one of my favourites, Romans 12:2 (NLT): Don't copy the behaviour and customs of this world, but let God transform you into a new person by changing the way you think. Then you will learn to know God's will for you, which is good and pleasing and perfect. So, fix your eyes towards Heaven!

PRAY

Lord Jesus, help me to look to you. May I not be distracted by worldly things, but look to the things of Heaven. Transform my mind that I would have a different perspective, which would lead others to Christ and not to the world. AMEN.

19

DAY 8 : NOTHING LASTS FOREVER!

Have you ever noticed how things don't last very long in this life? I thought so. I was really looking forward to having my central heating replaced. The timer unit was broken, the boiler made weird noises and the hot water cylinder sounded like a rocket! I had just put my French fries in the oven and that sounded like it was going to go bang too. I stood there and laughed to myself, and thought, 'nothing lasts forever'! Not money, relationships, possessions, time on Earth, nothing!

The bible says we should not look to things that are seen, but unseen. 2 Corinthians 4:16-18 from The Message version says:

So we're not giving up. How could we! Even though on the outside it often looks like things are falling apart on us, on the inside, where God is making new life, not a day goes by without his unfolding grace. These hard times are small potatoes compared to the good times, the lavish celebration prepared for us. There's far more here than meets the eye. The things we see now are here today, gone tomorrow. But the things we can't see now will last forever.

The small potato bit made me think of my French fries! The reason why I could laugh was because I know deep inside that something far greater lies ahead. I am not referring to a new boiler or oven, as useful as they are, but to the greatness of eternity. In the grand scheme of things, some of this earthly stuff doesn't really count for much at all.

The bible says we should not worry about tomorrow (Matthew 6:34). So, we look forward to the future whilst living in the moment.

That same day, I heard a song on UCB1 radio by Jeremy Camp, called 'Keep me in the moment'. It highlights some important lessons for living this life. Having our eyes wide open is to be spiritually alert. To be listening and looking for what God is saying in the moments of this life. To throw away what we are chasing after is to let go of the things of this world. Let's grab hold of all the goodness that God has for us as we wait for eternity.

Let's learn to grab the moments we are given and use them for God's glory!

Beautiful poppies on the local clifftops in Thanet

DAY 9 : LET YOUR LIGHT SHINE

I had the radio on and there was a gloomy comment about COVID being the worst pandemic since World War 2. I switched off the radio and at that point the Holy Spirit dropped this into my mind:

Will you be a light, will you shine bright? Will you penetrate the darkness?

What a challenge! The world for many people, including Christians, seems like a very dark place during a pandemic. Straight away I was reminded of a verse. Matthew 5: 14-16 (NKJV) says:

You are the light of the world. A city that is set on a hill cannot be hidden. Nor do they light a lamp and put it under a basket, but on a lamp stand, and it gives light to all who are in the house. Let your light so shine before men, that they may see your good works and glorify your Father in heaven.

It's an awesome verse which challenges us to be a shining light to those around us. And notice the bit about the basket, if we want to shine bright, we cannot be subtle about it. In a time of energy saving light bulbs, we often need more than one on to brighten up the room! We need to be flicking the light switches on in our lives.

We need to charge ourselves up with worship, with God's word, things of the kingdom. Then we need to share them, or SHINE them into the lives of others; including fellow believers. Some of whom can be more gloomy than those who don't have Jesus!

What the world needs now is hope, everyone has been impacted in some way. For many that hope may be the vaccine, or having a lockdown expiry date, or planning a future gathering or holiday! But if you have a faith in Jesus, NOW is the time to get shining and be the hope that people need, which will point them in the direction of God. John 8:12 (NLT) says:

Jesus spoke to the people once more and said, "I am the light of the world. If you follow me, you won't have to walk in darkness, because you will have the light that leads to life."

And that is our challenge. If we live for him, we need not be afraid of the seeming darkness that surrounds. And better still, we will shine his light into the lives of others so they can have it too!

DAY 10 : THINK, THANK, PRAY!

Quiet days mean you have less to do and more time to think. Our minds are so powerful and we can easily grab hold of a negative thought and let it take over. Whatever is going on in life comes to mind in the quieter moments. Be it finances, relationships, or work that needs doing at home, to name a few. What starts as a simple thought can then become something which changes our mood altogether. In some ways, that's quite frightening!

I got home to find a letter on my doormat. My credit card company decided to send me a default bill, albeit only £9, for a failed payment, even though my card was fully paid off. In reality, poor timing of a direct debit cancellation was the cause. I knew I would need to make the dreaded phone call to tell them I wanted the fee cancelled.

I find these things stressful! After going through about 5 menus of automated tripe, followed by a 40 minute wait (we are really busy, we care for you, thanks for waiting, blah blah blah!) I got through. The lady told me she could see my balance was zero and immediately offered the goodwill gesture of refunding the money. Just. Like. That. I didn't even ask for the refund, she just offered it, processed it and wished me a good weekend!

I know that's a small example, but it was still a blessing. Good things often come with a price, often it can be a long wait, or a painful experience, or something unexpected. But, good comes in the end! I am sure many of us have stories of struggle, of terrible worry and stress which.........turned out alright after all, or brought about a great blessing.There are countless bible verses on worry, anxiety and thinking. Here's just a few of them:

Philippians 4:6 (NIV): Do not be anxious about anything, but in every situation, by prayer and petition, with thanksgiving, present your requests to God.

Luke 12:22 (NIV): Then Jesus said to his disciples: "Therefore I tell you, do not worry about your life, what you will eat, or about your body, what you will wear".

Proverbs 3 5-6 (NIV): Trust in the Lord with all your heart and lean not on your own understanding; in all your ways submit to him and he will make your path straight.

And finally, Philippians 4:8: Whatever is true, whatever is noble, whatever is pure, whatever is lovely, whatever is admirable - if anything is excellent or praiseworthy, think about such things.

Wow! Powerful instructions for living in every one of those scriptures. I guess that could be summed up with the phrase, 'Think, Thank, Pray'.

Think about what is positive and gives you hope. Be thankful for what you have and what may come. Pray, giving those thanks and making your requests before God. So next time you're worrying, ask yourself, do I really need to worry about this? Is this thought process giving me the hope of Jesus or just leading me down a dodgy path which isn't going to help me?

DAY 11 : FROM BROKENNESS TO BEAUTY & JOY

Joy is what I was feeling that day. With a new combi boiler, my shower now had pressure! It was wonderful, being stood under the hot water. I felt so thankful, I even shed a few tears of joy as I laughed happily at the difference in water pressure! I also thought about how long I had waited for that moment, a year and half in fact. I had under-estimated how much that simple thing had affected my quality of life. Something once broken had now been fixed and it was well worth the wait.

That same day I was chatting online about human brokenness, regarding relationships and what 'baggage' we would accept. Much like material things go wrong and need repairing, so do we. But the complexities of human nature make it seem so much more painful. As I was thinking about it, the word 'baggage' struck me. It's rather negative, almost like we stigmatise ourselves with whatever we have been through that hasn't quite gone to plan.

It is my brokenness though which is changing me. It has caused me to question what I previously thought, whether attitudes, or expectations in life. I feel I have become more open and more compassionate. I am learning to laugh more, even by myself! Once I had started to write my Facebook blog (Sam's Life Encouragements) this book is based on, my anxiety significantly dropped

The point I want to make is that brokenness makes you beautiful. We need to stop using our negative past experiences as a way of labelling ourselves. We also need to stop labelling others.

My name is not 'divorce' or 'single' or whatever. It is 'Sam'. And I have my own story, just like you have yours. Brokenness eventually turns into joy and moments of joy can also be experienced during the healing process. The Message version of Psalm 30 verse 5 says:

The nights of crying your eyes out give way to days of laughter.

I love that. The Newsboys Christian band sings that pain comes in the night, but joy comes in the morning after. We also need to remember that we are not alone in our sufferings. Many others have probably faced the same, and Christ himself suffered the most brutal humiliation and death. But importantly, that is not where it stopped. He rose again. John 16:33 says:

In this world you will have trouble. But take heart! I have overcome the world.

Psalm 147:3:
He heals the broken-hearted and binds up their wounds.

So, be kind to yourself. Remember that your brokenness is not a label, but part of a process which is turning you into someone even more beautiful. I don't know how long the season will last, but like all things it will only serve it's time and then your joy will come.

DAY 12 : BEAUTIFUL SKIES AND HEAVENLY EYES

The weather in Kent had been beautiful! I had been all over the county that day and the sky was a wonderful clear blue. On the way home, I had to park up and have a walk by the sea. What struck me was the beautiful reflection of the sky on the water. Another name for the skies is the heavens, and it's like the heavens were being reflected back!

Have you also noticed how the sea looks dull and a different colour on a miserable day? It made me wonder what reflection I have in my life. When I am with other people, do I reflect something positive, do I glow and reflect heavenly things? One of my poems is about the skies:

'The eyes of Heaven'

Flying high on wings of love
Soaring around on clouds above
Floating through skies like an angel
I can never get enough

A viewpoint from Heaven that is so high
Looking from here I wonder why
I worry
When I know you're seated and ruling from above

You opened the gate, beckoned me through
Seated me down, right beside you
Opened my eyes so I had a chance
To see things the way that you do.

Seeing things 'from above' gives us a different perspective. A challenge for us all in a world which focuses on the horizontal (earthly) and often denies the vertical (Godly, heavenly). I had moments that day when I was frustrated at other drivers, or simply had a good moan about the things that irritated me with a colleague. But what we need to do is learn to embrace a different viewpoint. One where we gaze Heavenward and learn to look at earthly things from a different viewpoint.

Psalm 19:1 says:

How clearly the sky reveals God's glory! How plainly it shows what he has done.

That verse obviously speaks about creation, but I think it goes beyond that. If we look to the beautiful skies, perhaps we will gain more heavenly eyes?

DAY 13 : KEEP WALKING

I was out for a walk and it was dry with a very cold breeze. As I continued the weather turned and snow was pelting against me in the wind. I was getting soaked, but I carried on. As my trainers were getting covered in sand, my jeans were rapidly getting wetter and the durability of my coat was being tested, it got me thinking.

I had chosen to carry on despite the conditions. I could have decided that it was all too much and got back indoors as quickly as possible. And there was my God given analogy for life. Sometimes we have to carry on, and that can often mean a deliberate choice to do so. Earlier on during that walk I had prayed and asked God if there was anything he wanted to say to me. It was once I had chosen to continue that I felt him speak.

As I walked up one of the footpaths, the lyrics of a worship song Cornerstone, by Hillsong came to mind, about Jesus being the Lord of all through the storm. Later on it refers to Christ as our anchor in a stormy gale. What a great reminder that God is in control. Whilst things around us frequently change like the weather, we have an anchor who holds us securely.

Isaiah 43:2 (ESV) says:
When you pass through the waters, I will be with you: and through the rivers, they shall not overwhelm you; when you walk through fire you shall not be burned, and the flame shall not consume you.

Philippians 3:13 from The Message says:

.........but I've got my eye on the goal, where God is beckoning us onward - to Jesus. I'm off and running, and I'm not turning back.

So remember that he is with you and keep walking!

The footpath heading towards Botany Bay

DAY 14 : WHAT'S IN YOUR BOX?

A shipping container on the promenade got my attention. I loved the turquoise colouring and I found it's rustic nature quite appealing, but also the bright buoy right next to it. Then God gave me the phrase 'what's in your box?'. The box represented the heart, in the spiritual sense.

We will all have many things in our box, ranging from horrid things we don't like to talk about to great gifts yet to be released to the world. Our hearts are unique and complex. Much like a shipping container, things go in and out of the heart.

I couldn't help but remember news stories of immigrants in shipping containers and how in the same way there are things we need to let go of or want to escape from in life. I thought about how containers go through customs processes and how in the same way, we need to regulate what goes in and out of our hearts and minds.

I then looked up buoys and the colours have meanings, yellow means it is a cautionary marker. It is to warn of something to guide a ship. So the warning marker (the buoy) was next to the heart (shipping container). This made me think of Proverbs 4 v 23 which tells us to guard our hearts above all else because everything we do flows from it. How beautiful that those representations were placed right next to each other like that!

The bible tells us that God does not look at the outward appearance like people do, but he looks at the heart (1 Samuel 16:7). It also tells us that we will find God when we seek him with all of our heart (Jeremiah 29:13). I am sure you will agree with me that our desire and prayer should be this:

Create in me a pure heart, O God, and renew a steadfast spirit within me (Psalm 51:10 NIV).

The shipping container and buoy on the walk

DAY 15 : MAKE YOUR MOMENTS MATTER!

I went to the hospital to pick up a blood pressure monitor, as part of a series of tests to investigate my heart palpitations. The arm cuff inflated every 30 minutes as the monitor took a reading. I was struck by how quickly the time passed between each inflation! It made me think about what I do with my time and how many months had passed waiting for the monitor.

What we do with our time is important, particularly when it goes so quickly. Ephesians 5 v 15-17 in The Living bible says:

So be careful how you act; these are difficult days. Don't be fools; be wise: make the most of every opportunity you have for doing good. Don't act thoughtlessly, but try to find out and do whatever the Lord wants you to.

The other moment which stood out on that day was a conversation with a contractor at work. I had mentioned my palpitations and he said he had them too. I found out he had lost a relative recently and had been through a divorce like myself. Chances are likely we had similar stresses affecting our mortal bodies! I came away from that conversation believing God had allowed it to happen. I have since prayed for that guy and hope the holy spirit makes a difference in his life through what we shared.

I liked that conversation for two reasons. There was a sense in which I felt less alone in my problems, we all suffer in some way. But also that it took the focus off me for a while too. The Living Bible, Philippians 2 v 3-4 says:

Don't be selfish; don't live to make a good impression on others. Be humble, thinking of others as better than yourself. Don't just think about your own affairs, but be interested in others, too, and in what they are doing.

So one way we can spend our time wisely is to invest in others. Perhaps you can be a listening ear for somebody, give someone some encouragement, or bless them with a present.

There are so many verses on time passing by, some of which are a bit sombre, so I am finishing with one of the slightly more cheery ones! Psalm 90 v 12 (NIV) says:

Teach us to number our days, that we may gain a heart of wisdom.

I think that puts time into perspective nicely. I am definitely up for using my time wisely if I can get some wisdom out of it!

Be blessed as you bless others, and make the moments matter.

DAY 16 : MIGHTY WAVES

The waves were fascinating that day. I just stood there and watched them, with my camera at the ready, waiting to grab the moment. It was cold and wet but I didn't care, I was lost in the moment. I smiled and laughed as the waves crashed against the shore. I will never ever tire of the sea and it's majestic power and that beautiful sound it makes which satisfies the soul. I felt inspired to write the following poem when I got home.

Mighty Waves

Like the raging of the seas
Is the power of your mighty hand
I feel your love rushing over me
Like waves crashing into the land

As I gaze upon the waters
You satisfy my soul
Like the moon and the sun guide the tides
I know you are in control

Oh how majestic you are
God who created the waves and the shore
As I experience your mighty power
You leave me calling out for more!

Next time you're by the sea, take a moment to embrace its majesty, which leads us to the one who made it!

Reflect

Even though the fig trees are all destroyed, and there is neither blossom left nor fruit; though the olive crops all fail, and the fields lie barren; even if the flocks die in the fields and the cattle barns are empty, yet I will rejoice in the Lord; I will be happy in the God of my salvation. The Lord God is my strength; he will give me the speed of a deer and bring me safely over the mountains.

Habakkuk 3 v 17-19 TLB

My favourite photo from my trip to Austrian Tyrol

DAY 17 : I AM NEVER ALONE

It was early in the morning and some lyrics had come into my head. They were the words from a Justin Bieber song called Anyone, where he sings about his love for one person and not anyone else. Unlike Justin who is married, I don't have a fellow human to sing a love song to. It is something that I long for every day. But in this season, actually even in those where I may be in love one day, my focus needs to be on someone else.

It needs to be on the one who placed me here. It was 5:24AM when God woke me up to reveal the original message for this encouragement. The reality is simple, if God wants to share something with me, it's his timing and not mine! When I feel that nudge, I respond and would be foolish not to. Upon waking that day God gave me the words of this poem:

In you I believe

As I lay awake in bed with thoughts in my head
It's easy to feel like I am alone
But as I think about all you have done
I remember that I am never on my own
What's the point in chasing after things of this world
When I can chase after the things of your word
Your promise is that you are with me
And I don't have to do it on my own

In you I have my security
When I think about all you have said
Your promise is that you will guide me
And shine a light on the path that's ahead

So I lay it all down again for youLeave my burdens
at the cross
So I can embrace everything that you have for me
Even though it has come at a cost
So here I am with open hands
I am ready to receive
Reveal to me the master's plan
In you I believe

As I walked one day, I loved the way the sun was
shining on the cliff face and had to take a photo. I
know now that picture was meant for this word.
Psalm 119:105 says God's word is a lamp to our
feet, and a light to our path.

Perhaps you feel alone sometimes or you wonder
what God is doing. It can sometimes feel like there
isn't much light on the path. But a God who wakes
us up in the darkness to speak must be up to
something. So pay attention, heed his word and
look for the light shining on the path!

Beautiful sun shining on the cliffs at Foreness Point.

DAY 18 : ONE STEP AT A TIME

I was walking and had all sorts going through my mind. More specifically, I was reminded of places I have been in my life up until that point. The steps in the photo reminded me of an outing to Folkestone, the wintry Ramsgate harbour of a holiday to Iceland and some of the architecture of trips to continental Europe. Each of those trips and the emotions and experiences they entailed were steps in my life, which have contributed to making me the man I am today.

Amusingly, on my return part of the walk, I hit a dead end. Literally part of the prom which stops dead so you cannot go any further unless the tide is out, which it wasn't! So I had to turn around and walk back a few minutes before ascending the steps up to the top of the cliff. I laughed at myself, I should have remembered that bit, but had left it too late!

It made me think of life and how sometimes we may have to go back a bit to go forwards again. Perhaps we have to deal with some of the previous steps so we can progress. Or maybe we repeat the same steps as we are growing. I have a small wall plaque in my hallway, right before the stairs which go up into my maisonette. It's similar to a well-known quote by Martin Luther King Jr. The quote is

"Faith is taking the first step, even when you don't see the whole staircase".

As we go through life we cannot see the future. We can physically see what's in front or may have a plan, but we cannot see ahead in time. Only God can see that, which is why we only need faith for the first step. He rarely gives the whole picture, I'd even suggest never! When God reveals a poem to me for example, the Holy Spirit reveals it to me line by line, or a step at a time.

On the final part of the walk, I was pretty tired. I'd walked for over 2 hours and could feel my legs aching and I was getting hungry and thirsty. Life can often feel like that and when it does, the steps can often feel so much harder. But the reality is I did not have to rush back. I slowed my pace a bit and made sure I continued to enjoy the journey.

And that is what we need to do with life. Maybe you are struggling with where you are right now, or how things are. Remember to make the most of where you are on the journey. Take the opportunities provided by God to slow down and take notice. You only have to take one step at a time.

The staircase near Ramsgate, after my U-turn!

DAY 19 : UNCOMPLICATED

That word is the title of a beautiful song by Hillsong Young and Free, the acoustic version is wonderfully….uncomplicated! It is a beautifully stripped back song. It is about the simplicity of God's love for us.

We often over complicate life, whether it's our general level of busyness with work or social life, or during recent COVID days, cramming in online meetings and fretting about the housework or educating the children. We can easily become trapped worrying about current circumstances. We over think things, but we are better off slowing down, embracing the moment. And we have to be intentional with it.

I try to walk every day and take time to relax. To stop, to listen and to savour. But through it all, we must remember we are loved. YOU ARE LOVED. But the love we have from our father in Heaven is so much greater than a human could ever offer. Thank God for that!

The song talks about God's uncomplicated love for us, accepting us how we are. Also how he loves us simply even when we overthink. I think these words serve as a challenge and a reminder. Let's not make things more complicated than they have to be. Hebrews 12:1 from The Living Bible says:

Since we have such a huge crowd of men of faith watching us from the grandstands, let us strip off anything that slows us down or holds us back, and especially those sins that wrap themselves so tightly around our feet and trip us up; and let us run with patience the particular race that God has set before us.

The emphasis I want to take from that is not being held back. We all have our journey to finish. We have to strip back anything that clutters and gets in the way, like overthinking and worry.

It may seem contradictory in worldly terms, but when we are running the Christian race, slowing down will help speed us up. How? We will be able to see him and hear him more clearly, so we can move forward.

It's time to get uncomplicated!

Reflections at Kingsgate bay

DAY 20 : FEARFULLY AND WONDERFULLY MADE

The slogan for L'Oréal states 'Because I am worth it!'. I love that phrase because it is positive. Sadly that's what makes it stand out in a society saturated with negativity.

It was Valentine's Day, and for many it is a hard day. People on their own are quite frequently ignored by society, and the reality is that a commercial day doesn't really represent what true love is. As I woke that morning, some of the lyrics of a secular song came to mind from 'Afraid' by James Hype. It speaks of a fear of the night, of the loss of a relationship and even a fear of one's self! There are many people who feel insecure, and the loss of a relationship (like that in the song) is certainly one common cause. Unexpected twists and turns in life can make each day feel like a battle.

Battles for contentment, self-worth, recognition, purpose and of course love, are familiar to many of us. But we need to remember that there is hope! Psalm 139:13-14 (NIV) says:

For you created my inmost being; you knit me together in my mother's womb. I praise you because I am fearfully and wonderfully made; your works are wonderful, I know that full well!

'Fearfully' in the biblical sense has nothing to do with fear really; at least not like the worldly definition. The Hebrew refers to great reverence, heartfelt interest and respect. And wonderfully means set apart and unique. Whatever our relationship status, we are loved by our creator! We are created in God's image with great care and love. We must all try our best not to allow our relationship status to affect our view of God's love for us. Our confidence needs to be in God and not in the things of this world. I confess that I often struggle with living alone and my single-hood daily. This is a message for me as much as anyone else. Hebrews 10:35-36 says:

So do not throw away your confidence; it will be richly rewarded. You need to persevere so that when you have done the will of God, you will receive what he has promised.

How encouraging! We need to be confident in the one who created us and in the purpose he has for us. God has tasks for us to earn our heavenly reward, whatever our relationship status. Let's not forget that! God is working in us in our different seasons of life. Philippians 1:6 reassures us ....'being confident of this, that he who began a good work in you will carry it on to completion until the day of Christ Jesus.'

We are all a work in progress and whatever season you are in, we all have the same hope in Christ Jesus. As Isaiah 40:31 (NIV) beautifully puts it: 'but those who hope in the Lord will renew their strength. They will soar on wings like eagles; they will run and not grow weary, they will walk and not be faint.' Remember where your true hope lies. Because my beautiful friend, you are fearfully and wonderfully made!

DAY 21 : SHAPED INTO HIS LIKENESS

I woke in the early hours, about 330AM and I was pretty groggy. I'd been having a weird dream and then there was an irritating noise in my block of flats. Running an appliance at night is not cool! It got me awake and thinking.

The previous day I had walked past some cliffs and seen all the material that had eroded, as a result of the recent weather. Some of it had fallen down as I walked past. The cliffs were taking a new shape. I took the photo as thoughts about reshaping had come to mind.

I thought about rivers and the sea and how they both cause erosion. They can be gentle or powerful as they rub away, eroding the land alongside them. Over time arch ways can become stacks by the sea or new islands can even be formed by rivers. The lyrics of a worship song came to mind, reminding me of God as our strength and shield.

We have to be willing to allow God to do his business in our lives. He loves to reshape us and turn us into something better. And much like the erosion, sometimes it's gradual and slow, others it's powerful and comes with a bit of a thump!

I have to briefly mention Kintsugi, a Japanese pottery method. It's when all the broken pieces of pottery are repaired and are put back together using a lacquer mixed with powdered metal, often gold. The result is a stunning reassembled pot with all its imperfections on display. The 'scars' become

part of its beauty. Evidence that the potter has been at work! Isaiah 64 v 8 (NASB) says :
But now, O Lord, You are our Father,
We are the clay, and You our potter;
And all of us are the work of Your hand.

I have a scar on my head as a result of a minor operation. The hair will never grow back and the scar is pretty big. It's something I now have to live with. I vividly remember a nurse saying to me ' it's your new personal identification marker'. I love that! Whatever we go through, the resulting scars are now part of our story. They are evidence of what and who has made us the person we are today.

And as it's God who is reshaping us into his likeness, why not be pleased with those scars?!

Cliff erosion along the coastline near Cliftonville

DAY 22 : CHOOSE LOVE

I was driving to a location in North Kent for work and decided not to use my sat nav. I have been there plenty of times before and knew exactly what sign I had to look out for, so decided I would be extra vigilant for that sign. So what did I do? I drove straight past it and had to back track 10 miles with the help of Google Maps! I laughed at myself in the van and thought about how life is like that sometimes. We can have the best of intentions and still go astray!

As I walked after work that day, I found myself singing lyrics from a song by Toby Mac called 'It's you'. It speaks of putting God first and everything falling into line and how he always holds our heart. As we are travelling along the road of life, even if we are not sure what direction we are headed in, we need to love him first. So, that should be our ultimate direction! Mark 12:30-31 (NLT) makes this clear:

And you must love the Lord your God with all your heart, all your soul, all your mind, and all your strength. The second is equally important: Love your neighbour as yourself. No other commandment is greater than these.

As we love God first and love our neighbours, we are putting ourselves in the best position to hear his direction. As the song illustrates, it's about having God as our priority, before the rest falls into place. We may not always see all the signs he gives along the way, but he knows our heart and we will get to the right place eventually!

John 14:6 says:

Jesus answered, "I am the way and the truth and the life. No one comes to the Father except through me.

And John 3:16:
For God so loved the world that he gave his one and only Son, that whoever believes in him shall not perish but have eternal life.

So Christ died to demonstrate God's love for us and to illustrate that Jesus is the way. If we do come a bit unstuck along the way, God loves us so much, he willingly steps in to help us out. And he has a lot more knowledge than Google does!

So if you're unsure which turning to take, or even feel like you missed the signpost altogether, choosing love is a great place to start!

Ramsgate on the same day as the U-turn walk!

A word fitly spoken is like apples of gold in settings of silver

Proverbs 25 v 11
NKJV

DAY 23 : A STRONG TOWER

I was feeling pretty low. The combination of lockdown and my current situation was definitely affecting my mood. I knew I needed to walk and as I set off I prayed and asked God to speak, knowing the pleasure I get when I hear his voice and the fulfilment of writing it down.

I can only describe what ensued as a prophetic walk, in which a 'story-line' unfolded piece by piece as the Holy Spirit spoke through what I saw. So please, join me on the journey.

I saw a boat, sailing around the shoreline, it looked like an RNLI one with its unmissable bright orange top and deep coloured bottom. Immediately I thought of the word rescue, and how people need rescuing. Not only from trouble on the waters in a physical sense, but also in a metaphorical one, as we can face stormy seas in life.

The lyrics of a worship song, 'Came to my rescue' by Hillsong, then came to mind about us calling and God answering and coming to our rescue. Much like a person in distress on the water cries for help, or a captain makes a mayday call, we can call out to God in our times of trouble. Sometimes we can find making this call difficult, wondering whether or not God has heard our plea for help.

As I continued walking and thinking, some different lyrics came to mind from 'Ship to Shore' by Chris de Burgh. It's about a fading mayday call and a cry for a signal to come home. I remember hearing it many times as I was growing up. The song appears to be written about a lover who's gone and is greatly missed.

In the same way, we call out to God when we want his attention. And no doubt he wants our attention too. Much like a desperate swimmer longs for a person's arm or the rope of the RNLI, we often long for the arm of the Father to reach out to us.

I continued walking down onto the beach. I looked at all the reinforcements around the coastline. Masses of concrete and bricks support the cliffs and help in the battle against erosion. I thought about how we can often feel weak or in need of support. Much like those cliff supports take a heavy weight, we can often have a heavy load and need reinforcements.

As I continued looking (at the section in the photograph shown) I was reminded of the lyrics of a song I sang at Sunday school, which are taken directly from a bible verse. Proverbs 18:10 (NIV) says:

The name of the Lord is a fortified tower;
the righteous run to it and are safe.

A different lyric by Chris de Burgh came to mind from the same song about a beacon bringing him bring him home. That verse in Proverbs provides us with the answer to that request. He is our strong tower and place of safety. Psalm 46:1 says:

God is our refuge and strength, an ever-present help in times of trouble.

Are you feeling weak? Do you need reinforcement? Maybe you have been sending out distress signals.

Then remember the truth inspired by those Hillsong lyrics, we call, He answers and He comes to our rescue.

PRAY

Father God, thank you that you are my rock and my strong tower. Thank you for being my help in times of trouble. Thank you that you hear my cries and you answer me. Help me always to depend on you.

Amen

Kingsgate beach – my reminder of a strong tower

DAY 24 : LIVING WITH DISCERNMENT

Sometimes we struggle to make a decision. Maybe we don't know what to do next or we are waiting for the feeling something's right. It's ironic that as I am writing this, I have been debating in my mind whether or not to. And what is the topic? Discernment.

I was walking on a hazy day and it was hard to distinguish the line between the sea and the sky. There are times in life when things feel cloudy and it's difficult to make out the line. The horizon reminded me of the phrase 'a fine line'.

To give an example, we know that it is biblical to let God be the ultimate judge of others. But we also know we should get alongside one another to help each other in living a biblical life. Galatians 6 v 1 (NIV) says:

Brothers and sisters, if someone is caught in a sin, you who live by the Spirit should restore that person gently. But watch yourselves, or you also may be tempted.

2 Timothy 3:16-17 (NASB 1995) says: All Scripture is inspired by God and profitable for teaching, for reproof, for correction, for training in righteousness; so that the man of God may be adequate, equipped for every good work.

So in this case we need discernment, because on the one hand we want the other person to be free to use their own spiritual conviction but on the other, if we say nothing, they may miss out on necessary correction.

Also pertinent was a seagull sat on top of the post, like it was on watch! In the same way, we need to be alert in our Christian faith if we want to be discerning. 1 Corinthians 16:13 (NIV) says:

Be on your guard; stand firm in the faith; be courageous; be strong

And Proverbs 2:11 says:
Discretion will protect you and understanding will guard you.

The Merriam Webster dictionary refers to discretion as 'the quality of having or showing discernment or good judgement'. So in line with that Proverb, the two elements of the photograph fit together. If we have discernment and understanding, we have protection and a guard. So as we walk our journey, let's do it with discernment!

DAY 25 : LOCKDOWN PROPHECY

It was stupid o'clock in the morning and again I had woken in the night. I had been up a little while. I did what I usually do upon waking and got out my phone, and listened to some worship music on YouTube. Having listened to a few songs I then attempted to go back to sleep. I couldn't settle and felt the Holy Spirit told me to stay awake.

God started to reveal a prophetic poem to me, so I got typing. This is what he revealed:

Society may be locked down
But I will lift you up
For my cup is overflowing
The church doors may be shut
But my goodness has not stopped
And my kingdom will keep growing
So lift up your eyes
Beyond things which are seen
Raise up your weary hands
And give honour to the king
Open wide your eyes
And let the light shine in
Can you not see
That I am doing a new thing
I want you to push through
Into the new unfolding story
The journey may be hard
But these times are revealing my glory
So arise, stand firm
Make sure that you're on guard
Arise, stand firm
For you know I have your heart
I am your God

And I am writing your story. We can't see everything that lies ahead, but sometimes God reveals a glimpse. We are curious beings and I believe that's part of our design. God wants us to be alert and forward looking as we seek to embrace the adventure that lies ahead for us.

Arch at Kingsgate Folly – Looking ahead

DAY 26 : IT'S TIME TO DROP YOUR LOAD!

As I walked I noticed plenty of ships out at sea. One particular ship was massive and it got me thinking about the load it could be carrying. A ship can often be referred to as a vessel and so can we.
As I was walking along the waters' edge I was reminded of the lyrics of a well-known worship song, 'What can wash away my sin?'

Much like a ship can carry a heavy load, we often do too! Perhaps we have a sin we have been battling with for a long time, or something that still bugs us from the past, that's not fully dealt with yet. The answer is in the hymn, the blood of Christ can deal with it!

When a ship starts its journey it is fully laden, with plenty of extra weight. At the end of its journey though, that load is deposited and so the ship returns much lighter. The captain would never expect to return his vessel back home with some of the load remaining on the ship! In the same way, our 'captain' wants us to deposit the weight of our sin on him, so we can journey with a lighter load. Matthew 11:28-30 (NIV) says:

"Come to me, all you who are weary and burdened, and I will give you rest. Take my yoke upon you and learn from me, for I am gentle and humble in heart, and you will find rest for your souls. For my yoke is easy and my burden is light."

The bible clearly instructs us to let go of our burdens. We all like a sense of control of things, perhaps that's why we find things hard to let go of. But, it is in our interest to release them to God. Psalm 55:22 says that if we turn our burdens to the Lord he will take care of us and never let the righteous person stumble. It is only once the ship is empty that it is ready to carry out the next task or journey prepared for that vessel; it is the same with us. 2 Timothy 2:21 (ESV) says:

Therefore, if anyone cleanses himself from what is dishonourable, he will be a vessel for honourable use, set apart as holy, useful to the master of the house, ready for every good work.

So not only do we have our load lightened, we are also prepared for the next part of the journey. Let's not hold onto anything longer than we have to. We need to remember that we are washed clean, can live lightly and have good works prepared ahead of us!

A short prayer

Lord Jesus, help us to honour you with our vessels. We give you our burdens and believe your promise of a lighter load. May we live in the freedom bought by the washing of your blood and be able to step confidently into the works you have planned for us.

Amen

DAY 27 : HOPE IN EVERY SEASON

I was worn out after a really busy day. As I walked up a slope from the beach to the clifftop I felt like I needed to put in extra effort to get up the hill! Amusingly it reminded me of the bible verses in Isaiah 40 v 30 (TLB):

Even the youths shall be exhausted, and the young men will all give up. But they that wait upon the Lord shall renew their strength.

I'd felt low for a few days, and I don't wear a mask for my feelings, I think we should be real about them. The combination of some drab weather along with the daily battle of living alone can take a toll. A pat on the back and a cliched Christian phrase is poor medicine in my opinion. We need to feed ourselves and each-other with the goodness of God's word and his love.

Whilst my encouragements are applicable to me as much as anyone, I know this one is particularly pertinent for all of us. We have been travelling through a season which has taken a toll on our mental health, amongst many other things. If I was to ask if you have felt low at any point since the beginning of the pandemic, no doubt you'd raise your hand.

The bible speaks of seasons. In Ecclesiastes 3 (KJV), the first verse says 'to everything there is a season, and a time to every purpose under the heavens.'

I am sure that you, like me, will be pleased when this current season comes to an end. Perhaps by the time you read this, it already has.

As I drove home from my walk, the lyrics popped into my head from the famous song 'You raise me up'. They are a reminder that there is hope. And we must remember to dig beneath the surface, to remind ourselves of the good things that happen in difficult seasons too.

The blog this book is based on, was birthed in a time of anxiety and brokenness in my personal life, and in the middle of a pandemic! Often we need these challenges, and even how they make us feel. God knows the right challenge of circumstances we need, to bring about his purpose in our lives. He is on our side and will help us in achieving his purpose for us. Philippians 2 v 12-13(TLB) says:

Dearest friends, when I was there with you, you were always so careful to follow my instructions. And now that I am away you must be even more careful to do the good things that result from being saved, obeying God with deep reverence, shrinking back from all that might displease him. For God is at work within you, helping you want to obey him, and then helping you do what he wants.

Let us all remember the greater purpose which we have been placed here for. Let's get alongside one another as the bible instructs us, to build one another up. For these things are only but a season and he is faithful to raise us up!

DAY 28 : APPLES OF GOLD IN SETTINGS OF SILVER.

As I wandered along the beach one afternoon, the sun had slowly started to set and was just hovering above the top of the cliffs. It make me think of a phrase I hadn't thought of for a while, 'never let the sun set on an argument'. I looked it up and in Ephesians 4 v 26 (NLT) the bible says:

And "don't sin by letting anger control you," Don't let the sun go down while you are still angry...

What we say is important. We live in a society where people easily get angry and this affects what they say. Whether ranting in the car towards another driver, shouting at a protest, or even engaging in arguments on the internet, words can be harsh.

As I continued walking I was reminded of some song lyrics by Matt Redman, 'So I'll let my words be few'. The song is about reverence to God in worship. But again, the part about words is what struck me; keeping our words few.

This does not mean we shouldn't be talkative, it means we need to think about what we say, ensuring we do not get too caught up in the moment. It's one thing if we are full of words of love, but quite another if we are angry and what is said becomes damaging and no longer representative of Christ.

It's saddening how much anger some people can show towards their own brothers and sisters who hold a different political opinion to them, for example. But as believers we should do better and set an example of love to others, including the words we speak.

There are some beautiful biblical proverbs about our speech, including these:

Proverbs 25 v 11 (NKJV):A word fitly spoken is like apples of gold in settings of silver.

Proverbs 16 v 24 (NKJV):Pleasant words are like a honeycomb, Sweetness to the soul and health to the bones.

Proverbs 21 v 23 (NKJV): Whoever guards his mouth and tongue keeps his soul from troubles.

The final thing which caught my attention was an empty whelk egg case. The tiny sea snails are deposited in the water and these cases are often seen washed up on the shore. It made me think of how our words are like seeds and the impact they could have.

These cases can hold hundreds of eggs, and in the same way the snails are birthed in the eggs and released into the sea, our words are 'birthed' in our minds and released into the lives of those around us. We need to be mindful of what we are releasing!

What have you given birth' to today? 1 Corinthians 10:31 (NASB) says:

Therefore, whether you eat or drink, or whatever you do, do all things for the glory of God.

The empty whelk egg case, on the beach

For the word of God is
living and active,
sharper than any two
edged sword, piercing
to the division of soul
and spirit, of joints and
of marrow and
discerning the thoughts
and intentions of the
heart.

Hebrews 4 v 12 ESV

DAY 29 : BUILT WITH PURPOSE

I reminisced as I looked through the photo album I had made from my trip to Cambodia with Mission Direct in early 2020. I came across some notes I had written, from when I spoke in one of the morning team meetings. So this encouragement is based on those notes!

We were staying in Phnom Penh, a very busy city. Like many places in Asia it was dirty and untidy. The traffic was crazy, with endless vehicles all over the place. And of course there were loads of people. The phrase which God gave me was 'beauty in the chaos'. I felt that it was the people who make a place.

Whilst we were out there, our main project was building a home for a local family. As I was bricklaying one morning in the glorious sunshine, one of the bricks caught my attention. It had a huge crack down it and was discoloured, making it stand out from the rest. I decided I still wanted to use it. It looked burnt and misshapen but could still be part of something beautiful!

We have all been through the fire, or times of testing. But God loves us so much that he can use us despite all our imperfections. Much like me still choosing to use that brick! He can use these things to achieve his purposes through us. At the end of this life, we will reap our heavenly reward at which point there is a testing of fire.

1 Corinthians 3 v 13 (NASB) says:

each one's work will become evident; for the day will show it because it is to be revealed with fire, and the fire itself will test the quality of each one's work.

The other thing which had stood out to me there was the amount of joy that people had! They had big grins on their faces and they knew how to have a really good laugh. The bible tells us that despite the trials we face, we can still experience joy. James 1 v 2-4 (NASB) says:

Consider it all joy, my brothers and sisters, when you encounter various trials, knowing that the testing of your faith produces endurance. And let endurance have its perfect result, so that you may be perfect and complete, lacking in nothing.

Even when we are going through the tough times, God still wants us to be able to experience joy. Whatever trials we are currently facing and whatever imperfections we may have, we need to remember that our identity is in Christ and his design for us. Psalm 139 v 13-16 (The Message) says:

Oh yes, you shaped me first inside, then out;
  you formed me in my mother's womb.
I thank you, High God—you're breath-taking!
  Body and soul, I am marvellously made!
  I worship in adoration—what a creation!
You know me inside and out,
  you know every bone in my body;
You know exactly how I was made, bit by bit,
  how I was sculpted from nothing into something.

Like an open book, you watched me grow from
conception to birth;   all the stages of my life were
spread out before you,
The days of my life all prepared
    before I'd even lived one day.

So whatever your imperfections or current
circumstances, you are loved and have a purpose!

A photo of the brick in my Cambodia scrapbook

Let the words of my mouth and the meditation of my heart be acceptable in your sight, O Lord, my rock and my redeemer.

Psalm 19 v 14 ESV

DAY 30 : CHASED AND EMBRACED BY THE KING

I had been thinking about my divorce. Much like any significant event in life we can wonder why things happen the way they do. It's common to have hindsight and difficult to comprehend reasons whilst in the midst of a trauma.

I believe we have a jealous God. He loves us so much that he will chase after us whatever the cost, because he wants us back. He craves our attention so we can hear him clearly and live the life that he intended for us.

I believe he chased after me. I believe he saw how my life was going with my marriage and he knew he had something better for me. It seems crazy but I believe he allowed my marriage to end. That doesn't mean I promote divorce. But God's love trumps human love multiple times over. And he wanted my full attention and was prepared to chase me down to get it!

It reminds me of the prodigal son story in the bible in Luke 15 v 11-32. The father welcomed the son back despite him running way, squandering life and money and feeling unforgivable. In fact they even had a celebration on his return home.

No doubt this illustrates that Jesus celebrates us when we acknowledge our ways and come back to him. His loving arms are of course always wide open ready to embrace us.

The song Reckless Love by Cory Asbury is about Jesus coming after us with a fierce love. Breaking down walls, climbing up mountains and tearing down lies. Even leaving the 99 behind to chase the 1, like the parable of the sheep in Luke 15 v 1-8.

In Ezekiel 34 v 11 it says the Lord God will search for his sheep seek them out.

And Zephaniah 3 v 17 (ESV) says:

The Lord your God is in your midst, a mighty one who will save; he will rejoice over you with gladness; he will quiet you by his love; he will exult over you with loud singing.

So not only does he passionately pursue us, he rejoices over us when he's got us back. Where human love fails, his love is never ending. The pain may be hard, but I am so thankful he chased after me and I am safe in his heavenly arms.

Whatever trials you are facing, you can be sure his arms are open wide and if he needs to, he'll come running after you!

DAY 31 : WALKING WITH HUMILITY

As I walked along the beach I noticed that the winter sand barrier had been flattened. Spring was on its way at last. Initially the phrase 'let your guard down' came to mind. But then it became 'let down your barrier'. Immediately I thought about one of humankinds biggest barriers, pride.

There is a verse I love from The Message bible about humility. Proverbs 29 v 23 (The Message) says, 'Pride lands you flat on your face; humility prepares you for honours'. There is a song written by Matt Redman about revival which says that God will come and bring healing to our land, if we are humble and pray. It is based on 2 Chronicles 7 v 14 (NIV) which says:

.... if my people, who are called by my name, will humble themselves and pray and seek my face and turn from their wicked ways, then I will hear from heaven, and I will forgive their sin and will heal their land.

It's a beautiful promise, if we obey it's call to action to pray and live with humility. I remember many years ago I was sat in a church group one evening. As we were worshipping the Holy Spirit led me to what is now my favourite section of bible verses.

Philippians 2 v 5-11 (NIV) says:

In your relationships with one another, have the same mindset as Christ Jesus:

Who, being in very nature God,
did not consider equality with God something to be
used to his own advantage;
rather, he made himself nothing
by taking the very nature of a servant,
being made in human likeness.
And being found in appearance as a man,
he humbled himself

by becoming obedient to death—
even death on a cross!
Therefore God exalted him to the highest place
and gave him the name that is above every name,
that at the name of Jesus every knee should bow,
in heaven and on earth and under the earth, and
every tongue acknowledge that Jesus Christ is Lord,
to the glory of God the Father.

We are called to live like Christ and to have an
attitude like Him. That means being humble. It
means allowing any barriers we have to be removed
by the Holy Spirit, with his help. It means being
obedient so we can let go of ourselves and grab a
better hold of him. Let's not be proud, but walk with
humility.

Thank you so much for reading 'Beauty in the Chaos'. I hope the devotions have uplifted and sweetened your soul!

Please feel free to read and follow my blog 'Sam's Life Encouragements' on Facebook.

If you have enjoyed this devotional, please spread the word about it amongst your friends and family.

Love and blessings, your brother in Christ

Sam Silcock

Printed in Great Britain
by Amazon